The Experience Of Being Human

The Person

Michael Alan Paull

LLL Communications, Inc.
Coral Springs, FL

Books By Michael Alan Paull

The Experience of Being Human:
(Three Volume Set)
WALKING THROUGH LIFE
TALKING WITH GOD
THE PERSON

A Collection of
Anecdotes and Personal Reflections
On Life

To Learn more about the author go to:
MichaelAlanPaull.com

Copyright © Michael Alan Paull, 2007. All rights reserved.

Without limiting the rights reserved under copyright reserved, no part of this publication may be reproduced, stored in, or introduced into a retrieval system, or transmitted in any form or by any means without the prior written permission of the publisher of this book. The scanning, uploading, and distribution of this book via the Internet or any other means without the permission of the publisher is illegal and punishable by law. Please purchase only authorized electronic editions, and do not participate in or encourage electronic piracy of copyrighted materials. Your support of the author's rights is appreciated.

For more information please contact the publisher.

LLL Communications
2900 University Drive
Coral Springs, FL 33065
LLLCommunications.com

Illustrations by Steven Left
Graphic Design by Kall Graphics: Babs Kall and Michael Wall

Library of Congress Cataloging-in-Publication Data is available on request.
ISBN-13   978-1-934580-02-8
ISBN-10   1-934580-02-3

Printed and Bound in the United States of America

FIRST EDITION: June 2007

10 9 8 7 6 5 4 3 2 1

THE EXPERIENCE OF BEING HUMAN
Introduction

To be human is to be fallible and imperfect. It is to be susceptible to the full range of feelings, strengths and weakness of which man is capable. In a strange and paradoxical way, the discovery of our imperfection is also the discovery of perfection. The means of making that discovery is awareness.

In the awareness and acceptance of our imperfection there is peace. Our humanness is neither divine nor merely an animal. It is not eternal, but, finite. It is that which we leave behind when we die. Then another and higher aspect of what we are takes over. Often overlooked and easily denied, it is the essence of living in the physical and the concrete. For some reason, our human imperfection seems to bring shame and guilt if it is exposed to our selves and to others. Its one great asset is the ability to raise questions and by questioning to look through its experience. Its singular great power is that of choice. If it is sensitive enough in the working of its spirit, it is compelled to look deeply within itself and at the same instance to look above and beyond itself.

We use our intellect to reason and interpret our feelings. We concoct rules for behavior and codes for conduct. We develop belief structures to gain control over our joys and sorrows, our passions and our struggles, and our strengths and weaknesses. In so doing, we often miss the true nature of being human. Being human means we are imperfect and fallible. At one and the same moment, within the experience of our human being, we are confronted with the extremes of our human existence. In experiencing life we are confronted with an internal prodding and an external provoking. Within each life experience there is the full range of feelings, strengths and weaknesses of which we are capable.

Exposed to ourself, the awareness of our human situation may cause us to silently cry out. In that cry you hear the sound of the finite, fallible and weakness of our person. And you can hear the spiritual nature of our person lift its voice and expectation beyond itself toward God.

My writings express my personal experience of being human. My experiences as an individual tell a story in which others can potentially identify themselves. Questions and observations about life, God, relationships and one's Self form a mosaic from which thoughts and feelings emerge.

Underlying all things are the dynamics of personal faith and hope. And, of course, the greatest energy both stated and unstated is that of love. Therefore, all three books begin with the seminal statement, "The Experience of Love."

And so, within the experience of being human, our person sings its song of faith, hope and love.

MICHAEL ALAN PAULL

The Person

Preface: The Experience of Love 1

The Neckace of Love 5

Hard Times 9

Sighs Too Deep for Words 13

The Alone Child 17

Ache is Greater than Pain 21

Happiness 23

Change 27

Receiving the Gift of Love 31

How Deep is Deep 33

Alone But Not Alone 37

Wandering 41

It Paused At The Doorway 43

How Do I Keep Myself – Myself 49

You're Becoming Clearer 53

About the Author 55

The Inspiration

A young woman was troubled. Recently divorced, she sincerely asked me the question, "What is love?." I struggled to answer the question and realized that while I felt it, I had never taken time to define or describe it. Inspired by the desire to answer her question, I sat down and in two sessions the words for "The Experience of Love" flowed through my pen and onto the paper.

Written over 35 years ago, I have found it to be a meaningful, if ultimately incomplete, description of love. Love is the core and foundation of all human experience and searching. So, it is the underlying backdrop for all of the books in the Experience of Being Human.

PREFACE
The Experience of Love

There is nothing more beautiful, nor more hard to define than the experience of love. Many things are called love, most of them limited and protracted. And yet, somehow in the searching of those courageous enough to look for it, something happens which alters their entire perspective of life. That experience is love. It is personal yet not isolated. It finds immense self-gratification yet it, paradoxically, spends its energy in giving. Words cannot introduce you to it for it is an experience, an experience between two people, an experience with your SELF and an experience with God. It is a mystery and a secret but to those who have experienced it, it cannot be contained. It is shared, it is felt, it is non-verbal, it is real — it is love.

Love is the expression, the communication of life itself,
    self-love reflected and shared.

Love is the majesty and complexity of humanness,
    limited yet infinite, imminent yet transcendent.

Love knows the soaring of heights and the humility of kneeling,
    a journey through the valleys and peaks of life's experiences.

Love is spent unconditionally, reckless of cost,
    finding its value in the giving itself.

Love stands sensitively connected to another,
    concerned over the who and the where of the Person.

Love is neither excluding nor possessing,
    a mutual affirmation of self and other.

Love is not the fantasy or game of people who play,
    those pretending at love.

Love is not the romance of ego projected,
    it seeks the person behind the mask.

Love finds its object in another,
    having truly loved one, discovering a love for all.

Love is God; God is love,
    an experience, a secret, a revelation.

Love is YOU; Love is I; Love is US;
    one, then two, then more till finally ALL.

The Inspiration

What came to me was a picture of different charms on a chain. The feeling was that they were different aspects of love. With this inspiration, I began to write what came to me. The result was a necklace with a series of charms reflecting love.

The Necklace of Love

How do I know that I am loved?
  With what strange charms does the magic of love
    form its necklace around my heart
  Each charm is distinctly different
    and yet . . . . . all are tied together in harmony

The *necklace of love* thus formed is strung by
  the demands of careful choice
    Every single piece is selected for its
      particular need satisfied
    One desire leads to another until the
      string of charms forms its necklace
    All strung together by the thread
      of a single, unique human life.

How do I know I am loved?
  I know by the nature and arrangement
    of the charms which form
      a necklace of love around my life

There is only one demand made by this *necklace of love*
  the demand that only I can choose the charms which make it up
    and only I can choose the arrangement which creates
      the beauty of their appearance.

And so . . . . . with careful hands I reach for the
  charms which tell me I am loved

The first charm I choose are *the eyes* which look upon my person
  I know I am loved by the gentle eyes which care to look
    beyond the surface and into my life
  Eyes which have no judgment

And then, the charm of *the voice* which addresses
   the ears of a frightened child
      I know I am loved when a quiet voice says that it understands
         . . . . . a voice whose tone quiets my fears

Another charm I choose is *the hands* which touch my body
   I know that I am loved when the hands
      that touch me bring me no pain
         . . . . . but rather, the comfort of healing
   a hand which removes the inner conflict
      and replaces it with peace

Another charm I choose is the unconditional love
of *a mother's breast*
   I know that I am loved when the milk which brings me life
      is given with no strings attached
         . . . . . a breast which gives me nourishment and
            lets me go when I grow into the ability to feed myself

And then there appears the charm whose symbol is
   the strong right arm with a fist powerfully made
      I know that I am loved when the discipline of my life
         stands strong and firm and unyielding
            . . . . . an arm which not only controls my young life
               but which also protects me from harm

The next charm is the dual figure of *a man and woman,*
   hand in hand, walking together
      I know that I am loved when someone comes
         to share the adventure of my life
            . . . . . and the lonely walk becomes a dialogue of discovery

Another charm is *a circle of children* who stand arm in arm
   I know that I am loved when the offspring of my life
      form a circle of love
         . . . . . the great expression of my love for them
            becomes the exact expression of their love for one another

The last charm chosen is the center medallion
    the point of focus which brings everything into harmony
        the symbol of the sun which reflects the dazzle
            of the light in whose presence it finds itself
    I know that I am loved by the eternal presence of God's love
        which brings its light and life
            A circle of life which never ends
                A light of fire which never goes out

And so I have ***my magic necklace***
    a string of charms around my heart

        ..... ***the eyes*** which bear no judgment
        ..... ***the quiet voice*** which stills my fears
        ..... ***the hands*** whose touch brings peace and healing
        ..... ***the mother's breast*** that gives me the milk
            of unconditional love
        ..... ***the strong right arm*** of discipline and protection
        ..... ***the man and woman*** who, hand in hand,
            walk together
        ..... the encircled arms of ***children who love***
        ..... and ***the sun of light and life***
            whose dazzling rays express the warmth
            of a necklace of love

How do I know that I am loved
    I know by the pieces I have carefully chosen
        to form ***the necklace of love around my heart***

The Inspiration

There was a period of about two years in my church which was very difficult. The turmoil produced a great demand on myself to function in a healthy and mature manner. The times were hard. Externally the upset was constant. Internally the upset caused an introspective look at reality. The experience produced growth and enhanced sensitivity for my person. As God would have it, the conclusion of that hard time brought with it peace and growth and richness to the church and to myself.

Hard Times

These are hard times
    hard because they are difficult
      hard because they are unpleasant
      hard because they are unsettled
      hard because they are real
Fantasies . . . . . dreams . . . . . dependency
    someone taking care of you
      floating . . . . . nebulous reality

The strange thing about reality
    is that it seems so unreal
      something happening and yet feeling so impossible
Why is it that pretense and illusion
    seem so comfortable

One of the blessings of hard times
    is that they bring you to the real
Perhaps that is why hard times are so hard
    because they are so real

But hard times can become a blessing
    they can become God's richest blessing
      When things are hard
      When decisions must be made
      When survival is paramount
It is then that games can cease
    Friendship is tested and becomes true
    Truth hangs over you and
      Honesty is king

Yes . . . . .
      times are hard
        difficult
         unpleasant
          unsettled
          and real
  But times are also good
      Sensitivity is being enhanced
        there is no place to hide

I am growing

The Inspiration

I have always felt a longing and an ache deep within myself. A deep feeling of loneliness and a need for contact. One day the feeling was so strong that I felt the inspiration to express what was going on inside my person. Sighs too deep for words. The deep cry of someone aching. Out of my heart flowed the words which described what I was feeling.

Sighs Too Deep For Words

Oh my . . . . . Oh me
    Sighs too deep for words
   The deep cry of someone aching
      Sounds for which no words prove adequate

There's something deep within me
   something that wants to express itself
     it's a sublime something
      beautiful in its sadness
       lovely in its aloneness

The grandeur of such inner urgings
   are their inexpressibleness
  The sweet nectar of what they convey
    can never be mere words
      for words are poor vehicles

Deep sighs
    need to be touched to be felt
   Deep cries
      need the intimacy of contact to be fully heard

The depth of what I feel
   flows out of life itself
     a never ending stream
They are the discovery of my never ending person

If you hear my sighs too deep for words
    Can you respond
  The prize for your sensitivity
   is the gift of my person
      not the surface contact of superficialities
     but the deep inner meeting
      of person with person

Perhaps the reason that I sigh so deeply
      is the loneliness of my deepest parts
         It's the place where my life flows most
  If you enter my life at its source
         you shall surely taste its sorrows and aloneness
           but you will also taste its beauty
            and its loveliness

Reach out and touch me
     Let me touch you

Oh me . . . . . Oh my
     Sighs too deep for words
    The sighs of a person filled with love

The Inspiration

I have never met or known my father. The deep pain of feeling unwanted and abandoned left the child within me with an alone feeling. Over time the feeling of being alone has blended itself into the mosaic of a person made richer because of its total experience of life. This writing reflects a moment in my thirties when I made contact with that part of myself and felt inspired to allow the words to flow. Words which helped my emotions see myself more fully.

The Alone Child

Feelings with no feelings

There's something I've touched
   down deep inside me
  but it has no emotion
    just a heavy ache

I must have arrived at my innermost core
   the place where there are no defenses
     the painless pain
       the agony with no emotion
         the place of heavy sighs with no relief
        the place of quiet tears

What is it that needs such radical protection?
   Is there a bank of forgotten memories?
     A child's feelings better buried than exposed?

Questions with no proper answers
   Just a feeling with no words or emotions to explain it

I'm alone again
   this time it's alright
    no manipulations
 Alone with myself
   A Self of the alone child
    A child adrift in a sea of humanity

There are no parents to help this Child
   no one wise enough to understand
     no one capable of absolute empathy
       no one adequate to share the burden
The inner Child alone with its essence

The only pathway into this Child
 is the one forged by itself
 And when a child helps others to help him
 he no longer stays a Child
 The Child becomes the parent

Helping others to help yourself
 is too frustrating
 too fatiguing
 too fruitless

So its better to be alone
 Alone with your Self
 It's easier on the vital energies needed for survival

Perhaps sometime in those rare and vital moments
 Someone will reach in and make contact
 Then the Child can remain as it is

For you see . . . . . When the Child helps others to help him
 He ceases to be the Child
 He becomes the parent

———⚘———

The Inspiration

I was feeling something in myself that the concept of pain seemed inadequate to describe. It was greater than pain and it ached. I felt moved to describe what ache was like. So, these few words about pain and ache were written.

Ache Is Greater Than Pain

Ache is greater than pain
    It hurts more
  Pain is a place
    a location in the arena of human life
  Pain is something you can reach and touch
    a place to put your head
      a symptom leading to the cause
        a physical body healed and made peaceful

But alas . . . . . an ache is a hard place to find
    It is everywhere all at once
      And yet . . . . . illusive to the touch
    An ache is the hidden Self
      filling your body
        and yet never contained completely within it

An ache hurts more
  because its relief lies deep within the heart
    and the heart is the doorway of life

As life is greater than the body
    ache is greater than pain
  An empty place
    It hurts more

The Inspiration

A lady in my church insisted that everyone be happy. "Are you happy?" she constantly asked me. I asked her if she knew how to define or describe what being happy meant. She couldn't put words to it. Feeling challenged to define or describe happiness, I wrote these words. I was at lunch with my wife and in the midst of ordering a quiet voice told me to write about happiness. So, taking a handful of napkins, I wrote what came to me.

Happiness

Is it possible to be happy
    I mean really happy
Is there a state of being properly named Happiness
   a condition of mind and heart and body
     exactly known in experience
Is the search for Happiness simply a Shangri-la
   better known in fantasy
     as the Eden on the other side of the far mountain
Is Happiness a place only dreamed of
    never to be reached

But – ah! – my soul tells me that Happiness must be
    or else Life would not be balanced
   Like a light swallowed in darkness
    Hope would be lost in gloom
Oh – Yes! – just as night demands day
    So Life demands happiness

Perhaps the search for Happiness looks
    toward the wrong direction
  If you reach toward never-never land
    it proves unreachable
   If you look away from where you are
     your eyes have turned from its presence

For you see . . . . . Happiness is not far away
    for it is all around you
  Happiness must be accessible or it is only an illusion
If it is only an unreachable dream
    then it becomes a curse

But it is not a curse . . . . . it is a Blessing
    And a Blessing is always right at your fingertips
  A Blessing is always the Presence of Divine Love
    seeking your invitation

If Life is to make any sense
    If it is to have any order – any balance – any harmony
      Then Sadness is the sister to Happiness
        It is waiting to be discovered
          by a simple gaze
            a turn of the head
              a quiet recognition

Yes – Happiness is not an illusive city
    reached by a toilsome journey
  Happiness is where you are, surrounding you
    and waiting for recognition
In fact – Happiness is actually within you
    Looking for it you failed to recognize its presence

Happiness is a choice which frees the energy of your heart
    to shine its light on your life
Like the great Mysteries of Life
    Happiness was with you all the time
   Like all the great Mysteries of Life
     Happiness only needed
        the discovery of an awakened awareness

The Inspiration

During some hard times, I felt the need to relate to people and come close to my friends. In the midst of that need I reached out to people and found them changing. Instead of predictable relationships, I found the unpredictable fact of change. I found that you can't hold on to change. It doesn't stand still.

Change

My . . . . . how times change
     Goodness . . . . . how people change
   Calmness gives way to unrest
       Clarity to confusion

God's timing is interesting
   We all need people at one time or another
     We need their presence
         their thoughts
        their stability
          their understanding

But have you ever tried to hold on to someone
  who is spinning
     They're too hot to hold
       Their motion makes you dizzy

It's strange how things change
  Yesterday everyone seemed at least somewhat stable
    Today they bounce in fitful fashion
   Yesterday those close to you seemed open and responsive
     Today they appear closed and distant

It's strange how things are
  Friends want to give
     but don't know how to share
  But they're good people
    those that surround you
     It's just that they're so unpredictable

Maybe that's the way it should be
because that's the way it is
Ultimately you are left with just yourself
Your own strength
Your own stability
Your own opinion
Your own love

The Inspiration

Love is a gift that demands reception. Reception is easily fooled. Knowing this I have always felt the dilemma of trust. Reflecting on that fact, I wrote the words that were simple and direct. The conclusion is something that I have carried in my thoughts since then.

Receiving The Gift Of Love

When people want to give to you
    It usually has two sources
        Either they give in order to get something
           in return
        Or they give because they love
           Such giving is free and unconditional

Our problem is to know the difference
    We can be fooled

        We receive because we think it is love
           and find the giving had nothing to do with us
               It was all about the other person

        We refuse to receive because we don't trust the motivation
           and miss the love we so desperately want

What we need are eyes to see the truth
    What we need is a heart that is not afraid to feel vulnerable

The Inspiration

The relationship between my wife and myself was new and fresh. It was instantly filled with deep feeling that was to grow and grow. In that beginning we were caught up in what had begun to happen but were unsure of where it was going. Sitting with a group of people at a restaurant, I was moved by that fact. Inspired by the moment and the situation, I turned a placemat over and wrote the words that described our circumstance. Quickly finishing it, I handed it to the person next to me to give to her. It has proved to be a special writing for both of us.

How Deep Is Deep

How deep is deep?
    How true is real?

How much can a person experience another?
    As much as to move you within
        and beyond the limits of time and space?

To experience so deeply
    is to love in agony and ecstasy

        Can love ever be fulfilled?
            Can two people ever find the allowances of union?

Two become one
    and yet remain separate
  Two remain separate
    and yet forever coming together

      Ah . . . . . aloneness
        the price of discovery
      Potential never realized
        Life never lived

      Hope . . . . . loss
        warmth . . . . . emptiness
          two . . . . . one
            together . . . . . alone

      Life . . . . .
        too precious to give away
      Love . . . . .
        too essential not to be sought after

Love and Life
    silently shouting . . . . .
        deep
            true
                real

I must forever search
    whether or not I find or am found

        Don't weep . . . . .
            I know you're there!

The Inspiration

Before we were married, my wife and I experienced a love that grew deeper and deeper. Being apart touched that alone feeling that I have always carried with me. However, the love that I felt from my wife touched that part of me that felt alone. It was filled with the fact of its presence and the promise of it's fulfillment. Caught up in the strength of that deep feeling, I felt inspired to express myself.

Alone But Not Alone

I'm alone again
    but not alone

There's someone I love
    who loves me
        with a love that ties an umbilical knot

It's not a frothy kind of love
    a dreamy . . . . .
        sticky kind of fantasy love

It makes me feel attached
    even when distant

There is a warmth and depth
    and glowing beauty

But it aches . . . . . oh how it aches
    deep inside me
        in chambers where my spirit echoes
            its solitary presence

I'm alone down deep inside my being
    But I'm not alone anymore
        The vibrations of your love
            The promise of your person
                This makes me know I'm not alone

But I miss your touch
    the warm glow of your eyes

You are there . . . . . you know
    down . . . . . deep inside of me

    But its lonely . . . . . there
      down . . . . . deep inside of me

        Part of me is missing
          and I ache

What I have is the real and essential
    What I'm missing is the complete and perfect

So . . . . . I'm alone again
    but not alone

The Inspiration

For a brief time in my thirties, I found myself taking time to be alone. I would wander around downtown Chicago, my home town. Little did I know when I penned this writing I was being prophetic. You see, soon after writing it I met my wife and the writing was fulfilled. I found someone to hold my head, someone to feel close to.

Wandering

I'm wandering again

This time I'm not searching
    Just wandering
        Just restless

My soul is looking for a resting place
    You see . . . . . I'm tired

I just need somewhere to rest
    Someone to hold my head
        Someone to feel close to

I guess I just need you

So . . . . . I'm wandering again

The Inspiration

A common experience for me is the desire to make contact with another person and feeling the frustration of it not happening. The opportunity for real contact is a rare moment. If that moment passes without its fulfillment there is no certainty of it presenting itself again. Faced with just such an occurrence, I felt inspired to describe what I am certain is true for everyone.

It Paused At The Doorway

It paused at the doorway
    of sharing and revealing

Unable to take the fateful step
    that would begin the tender unfolding
        of person with person

    The sharing which would dare
        to bare
            the secrets
                which
                    though untold
                        are waiting to be known

Why is it that personal unfolding
    is so fearful and fragile

What is it that feels so vulnerable

Why do we so easily create barriers
    when what is waiting to be revealed
        wants so desperately to be seen
            and understood
            and known
                and loved

*Why so much fear
    and mistrust
        and doubt*

*Why can't we risk
    and expose
        to be seen
           who we really are
              what we feel
              what we think
              what we hope*

*Why can't we risk
    to express
        our fears
        and hurts
        and pain
        and joy*

Opportunity was there
      in one of its rare and wonderful moments
    It paused at the doorway
        of sharing and revealing

Two persons standing at the
    threshold of that rare moment
Unable to take the fateful step
    that would begin
        the tender unfolding of person with person

And so, opportunity passed by
    and the doorway of sharing and revealing
        was closed

Will it ever return

A hard question to answer
    for it is a fateful and rare moment
        when the spirit is present
            and two persons are open
                and in such sweet contact

If it does not, then there will be grief
    For the sharing which would
        bare
            the secrets
                will be untold
                    and unknown
    And who we really are
        and what we feel
            and think
                and hope
            will not be seen

And our fears
    and hurts
        and pain
            and joy
    will be unopened
        and remain unexpressed

But in the loss of opportunity
    may we hope
        – for a time
            when two persons
                may again feel fearful
                    and fragile and vulnerable

        – and the doorway
            of sharing and revealing again appear

The fateful step be taken
    and the tender unfolding of
        person with person
        make its contact of love

The Inspiration

My son asked me questions about relating to others without mixing yourself up with them. How do you maintain the integrity of your own feelings while mingling with the feelings of another? How do we keep ourself — ourself and let others be theirself? These questions were on my mind when, sitting on an airplane, I took a pad of paper and wrote what came to me.

How Do I Keep Myself – Myself

How do I keep myself – myself
    What must I do to let you be you

The confusion over what I am feeling
    – Is it what surrounds me that I experience within myself
    – or is it what I have projected upon my experience

Not easy questions to answer
    surrounded by a myriad of people and emotions
        – can I distinguish where I end and where others begin

Is the blurring of what I feel inevitable
    or can it be a solution waiting to be discovered

It's not so easy to relate to others
    if we project forgotten traumas of childhood upon
        our circumstance
        – for then we confuse our response and reactions
        – we color others with an emotional hue that more properly
            belongs to us

It's not easy to relate to others
    – if we transfer to them our emotions
        which more properly belong to someone else
            – the someone else that we avoid dealing with
                because of pain or discomfort or other reasons

It's not too easy to deal with others if we cannot pause
    – and put our reactions aside
    – and listen to them
        simply
            and clearly

When pausing in just such a manner
>   we must be cautious

It's not so easy to relate to others
>   If we take upon our shoulders
>   – their emotions
>   – their concerns
>   – their woes

If we do that
>   – We rob them of their burden
>   – We interfere with their journey in life

>   A journey in life in which God brings
>   to people just what they can handle
>   – so that they may grow and develop and evolve
>   It's easier to relate to others
>   – when we bear our own burdens
>   and let others do the same

It's easier to relate to others if we know ourself
>   – if I recognize what belongs to me
>   and what belongs to others

———∞———

The Inspiration

In experiencing the relationship between my wife and myself, many things have transpired. One of them occurred early in our relationship and has continued ever since. A mutual relationship that has total clarity and real contact.

You're Becoming Clearer

You're becoming clearer!

I'm used to fuzzy kinds of relationships
    the tepid kind that never seem to focus

Occasionally there comes to view
    Someone warm and exciting

But on the way in . . . . .
    they seem to cloud a bit
        become vague and shadowy

And so you back them up a bit
    to the point of comfortable focus

However . . . . . in your case my friend
    my dear . . . . . sweet . . . . . lovely friend
        the closer you come
            the brighter you become

On the way into my person
    you pass that magical point
        the point where the body ends and the Spirit begins

And . . . . . then
    I see you in your reality
        the beauty of what lies within

And I find the place where true love begins

ABOUT THE AUTHOR

Michael Alan Paull is an ordained minister. Retired, he is presently focused on his writings. The subject of these writings is the human being and the experiences which make up his life. The strong belief and the core of his philosophy is that the realized awareness of what it means to be human is the discovery of the context in which all human beings, everywhere, share in common.

The three volumes in this series about the "Experience of Being Human" are:

WALKING THROUGH LIFE

TALKING WITH GOD

THE PERSON

The several writings in WALKING THROUGH LIFE are a brief panorama of life. An experience of deep feeling and self transcendence.

TALKING WITH GOD is filled with questions and casual conversations with God. Thoughts and feelings filled with trust and hope and love. A human being in its finitenes experiencing the intimacy of the divine. A human being secure in its relationship of love with God.

The writings in THE PERSON are the introspective expressions of the self in the human situation. The experience of love finding itself within the depths of its own person and in its intimate personal relationship with another.